TANAKA

# FLASH IN THE PAN

ISBN 978-1-4477-5372-8

*"The mediocre teacher tells. The good teacher explains. The superior teacher demonstrates. The great teacher inspires."*

*For Daniel Smith, Alyson Martin and Sophie MacNeill. And for DLK, with love.*

# Contents

# Introduction

This book started life as a poetry collection. When I told a friend I was writing it he said that he didn't like poetry, but he'd buy it anyway. My knee-jerk, literature-loving-poet-worshiping response was that he *should* like poetry. But that's not right. Writers exist so that people can read them, and Flash in the Pan is, I hope, the sort of book that people who don't like poetry should pick up. It's more than just trying to treat flash fiction like the sugar for a bitter poetic pill. Life is poetry, language is poetry and the really great thing about flash fiction is that every sentence can be poetic without writing a poem.

That's the book I wanted to write, and that's why there are poems here, yes, and there are stories here too. This isn't a novella, a book of short stories, or a poetry collection.

This is Flash in the Pan, and it's for people who don't know they like poetry.

# Wet World

It was raining when I was born. I don't know this because I do not remember, but my mother told me, when she still told me things, that on that night she was crying, and my father was crying, I was crying, and God was crying harder than any of us. And now I think that maybe we were crying because we saw a little of what was going to happen and that God saw further than any of us, saw me, as I am today, and cried so hard that the river in our village burst its banks for the first time in decades.

An old lady died in that flood. Her little bungalow was next to the river and the water seeped in under doors and through cat flaps. She woke up, tripped and knocked herself unconscious, face down in the water. By the time they found her my mother had begun to love me, which took her a long time, and the old lady had putrefied in the filthy river water. In my dreams her face is a grey, decaying mask, with tatters of flesh clinging to yellow bones and her mouth is stretched tight in a skeleton's grin framed by lips which are black and swollen hideously, but she still has on her pearl earrings, and they are lustrous in the murk.

This, of course, is ludicrous; no one wears earrings to bed. But it's only imagination, which never did any harm to anyone.

It's raining now. God is crying. I'm not. I think he's crying for both of us, and his tears are soaking me through as I stand here, and in front of me the canal's surface is a patina of little ripples.

I don't believe in God. But I bet he doesn't believe in me either.

My first day of school, I cried. Second day I cried when I had to go home. I loved my first school. Mum had a thing for neutral tones at home, our house was all beiges and monochrome, and life there was a dull silence into which I was an intruder, overstaying my welcome, every inch the fat bawling visitor who never leaves. But school... there I felt safe. It was loud, it was noisy. The colours everywhere were bright, bold. Everything smelled and felt more alive. I remember that I would paint the palms of my hands with PVA glue and then shake them until it dried, like the translucent skin of some wet, blind, slimy underground creature taken from its subterranean lake. Then I would peel it off slowly, meticulously, luxuriating in each square centimetre of skin exposed to the air.

Such simple pleasures.

"Simple things please simple minds!" Mum used to say when she talked about me to her friends.

I don't mean to give the wrong impression of her. She was a brilliant, powerful woman. My father called her a Diamond, because it was her maiden name. His diamond. And she was. Charming, fashionable, a scintillating conversationalist, or so people described her. But to me the word diamond makes me think of diamond edged saws which can cut through anything, and sharp edges and harsh angles, or else of a poor soft lump of coal being suffocated to sparkling indifference in the bowels of the earth. That was mum. Every vestige of voluptuousness or excess was exorcised in favour of clarity. She was a model of prudence and precision. She could add up a string of four figure numbers in her head before anyone else could finish writing the first one down.

She always was a great businesswoman. She used to say that having me was the only career move she'd ever had cause to doubt.

But only when she thought I wasn't listening.

Growing up people always told me my future was bright. I could be clever when I wanted to be. I know what a blessing that is, but it doesn't do much good. Intelligence, beauty, talent, these are the consolations our parents provide us with to apologise for bringing us into the world.

Mine of course, apologised to me directly. I can hear my father's voice echoing in my head. "I'm sorry you were ever born." but I'm not too upset because this is progress, and the first thing we have agreed upon- the first proper conversation we've had-in years which means tonight we have taken steps in our relationship.

That wasn't very funny. I'm useless without an audience. Here, by this canal, I am useless.

But I can make people laugh a lot. I used to want to be a comedian, but I gave that up because I wanted to be an actor. They're not worlds apart, but I want to do serious work. And comedy is so much harder anyway- impossible after tonight, because I think I realised that laughing is like Christmas, or Yule, or Hanukkah, or any of the winter festivals.

Do you know why all the northern cultures had their own winter celebrations? Denial. Think about it; everything's cold, and the year is gasping its last breaths, and the world is dead or dying all around us, so we hang shiny things to catch what remains of the light. We drink ourselves into oblivion, and gorge ourselves on food and fuck ourselves into a thoughtless ecstasy because we can't handle the truth. And the truth, when all is said and done, is that the universe is cold, and huge, and doesn't give a fuck about a few billion fleshy sacks clinging to their little rock orbiting a speck of light at the edge of existence.

Rage, rage against the dying of the light.

And that's all laughter is. "Ha! Ha! Ha!" Just another pathetic little defiance in the moribund calendar of human endeavour.

Someone's going to think I'm insane. Standing by the canal, listening to the cars on the bridge above me and laughing- no- enunciating the syllables. "Ha Ha Ha." Laughing's a bit of an ask right now. I might manage a grimace if pressed, but there's no one here, and I had to climb over a fence to get down here anyway so I don't want to have to pretend to smile for anyone.

I sit down on the edge with my shoes off and dip my feet in the filthy river. I don't feel filthy though, just cold and numb. A shiver runs up my leg.

Some part of me, I think, must feel like crying. This is a fact, because something awful has just happened to me. Because of me. But I can't find it. Does that make me a bad person? I must be, because I can't manage to care that it's a possibility. There's a dead space where my conscience should be, and when I say that that's frightening I'm only saying the words.

I can replay the entire evening with marvellous clarity. I can see the moment my dad started shouting at me. I can see each of his eyelashes individually, and as he disowned me I counted the veins running through the whites of his eyes tiny red threads, or channels of mould through soft cheese, and there were six of them. Maybe I'm more like my mother than I thought after all.

I can remember the exact sound he made when I pushed him- a kind of whump and a sort of groan as he tumbled down the stairs, one hand scrabbling at nothing, until he was lying very, very still at the bottom with a crack in his glasses. I can remember that my mother gave a neat little gasp, and then screamed.

All this over a girl. Someone they didn't like. And yeah, they were right, because she turned out to be... well... she turned out to be just another Christmas bauble, and exactly as empty inside.

I don't blame her. I've done that. I've let girls fall for me while being totally and utterly aware that I don't give a crap about them. Ok, one girl. But if I pluralise her I make her into a type, and that's easier than calling her by her name.

I inch my way into the canal. It's not too bad, the cold burns, but then my legs go numb, bit by bit. It's not very deep I don't think. Too loud to be deep. Nowhere near deep enough to drown in. It's not raining hard enough for anyone to drown. Although, what is it they say? You can drown in a puddle if you lie face down in it.

If I were to drown in this canal they'd find me when I'd begun to decay, like the old lady who died as I was born, and my skin would be swollen and bloated with filth, but my teeth would still shine like her pearls in my imagination. I like that idea. That my teeth will be intact for a long time.

It would be very dramatic to kill myself. Mum would be in a kind of horrible ecstasy, and she'd grieve with such dignity that people would admire her even more, and then she'd just move on with her life. Because nothing gets that bitch down for long.

I step out of the canal. I'm not going to kill myself. I'm not going to go back. I'm going to wait until my feet and jeans are dry, and then I'm going to walk until I find something.

Something that matters.

# Spare Change

Beating the streets
with the flat of a foot
with a lack of inspiration

The world is waking, the sun tremulous and shy
caressing grey roads to ease the established chill
a woman in wrecked stockings stands by a Pret a Manger

brow studded and blonde, she asks
"Spare some change?"
I want to laugh: things rarely stay the same in London

Her voice is breathy, a nascent wheeze
I see the membrane between her nostrils
Has been assaulted; it is ugly red and sore

She is upset. I want to say something;
in my arrogance I long to make a gesture
Bought chips in a newspaper cornucopia

or some ridiculous cure-all saying.
But in this city you do not do such things
I pass her a pair of silver coins and keep walking.

# The Caricature

I saw a caricature of womanhood
bright as a neon balloon
and as vacuous

With acrylic mancatchers
stuck on her fingerends
and the stink of burnt hair

overlaid with Chanel or something pink
and the unmistakable air
of someone who Googles herself

she sways down the street
crushing Davison, Pankhurst and their ilk
with feet shoved into impossible heels

(No, it isn't fair, this judgement
she has lungs
she has hopes, concerns, capillaries
she is as human as me

and perhaps, as broken)

# Dear Joan

*Strange things happen in Paris's Centre Pompidou. This poem is one of them.*

Are they young men?
Are they old men?
Watching the way she
Turns. Turns.

Watching the way she
Burns and freezes
Bruised and bleeding.

Burn, burn
Joan-in-the-Fire
Strap down your breasts
they'll raise you higher

Jack-in-the-Green knows
You're no liar.

# The Wolf and a Bee

In India there are lots of jungles. Not as many as there used to be of course. The old places, holy green groves and sacred rocks where wolves congregated in their savage fora are few and far between. The place where Mowgli pinned Shere Khan's hide is probably in the basement of a MacDonald's now. The exchange of one holy space for another some might say, but I wouldn't listen to them.

But what of the wolves themselves? Like so many Indians of so called "noble" descent they have lost some of their grandeur. Food these days is scarcer, Man is more dangerous, and as the world turned, amidst fireworks, into the new millennium the she-wolves howled in fear at this new, irreverent epoch, where mankind lit up the sky as a challenge to the gods, and the he-wolves nosed at their cubs and nearly cried for terror at the bleakness of their futures.

Palli was one of those cubs, and little under a decade later, she found herself in a foul mood. This was not unusual- with less than two or three thousand of her kind left in the jungle gaiety was rare in her species, and even cubs these days have learned not to be too exuberant around their elders. Nevertheless, Palli was, to put it bluntly, royally ticked off. As a single mum in the harsh jungles of Rajasthan, life was a constant struggle. Food, discipline, territory, all the things which the Great Packs once took for granted were almost gone. Sure, you heard about the northern wolves, and their vast numbers but who'd be one of them? Or worse, the Americans.

These were the kind of things which passed through Palli's mind as she walked through the morning light. Around her the undergrowth pressed in, catching in her short fur and making her feel claustrophobic, nauseous. She could hear the humming of a hive somewhere, and the buzzing was assaulting her sensitive ears.

"Fucking bees!"

Ostensibly she was hunting, or at least that was what she had told the most responsible of the cubs when she'd left. Really though, she was just trying to get away from them. Yes she loved them, but all four were so...energetic. Dharshana was always asking questions, insatiably inquisitive, Kumeru was always lording it over his sisters and telling them tall tales, and the girls, Sita and Parvati were perpetually bickering. They *never* slept all at the same time, and to put it bluntly, they did Palli's head in. So she'd done something unusual. She'd gone out for a "hunt". In daytime.

The sun was shining- it was only dawn so not *too* bright- through the broad leaves, and Palli exulted in the soft sounds of the waking jungle. Peace.

You know, except for the bee. It had been following her, landing quite rudely on the place where her tail protruded, or just past her ears so that she jumped in surprise. At first she'd thought there were many of them, that she'd disturbed the hive, but no, it was the same one. It was almost *baiting* her, and finally, grudgingly, Palli decided to say something.

Of course, wolves seldom speak to insects. It's not *done*. Plus, if she was honest, Palli had always been particularly perturbed by bees- her den had been home to a large hive when she'd found it. Pregnant and desperate, she remembered attacking the hive and then leading the pursuing swarm into a nearby Man-village. Soon enough, of course, the bees were smoked out of the little cave, and Palli was able to move in and spend the rest of her pregnancy in relative comfort. Still, the burnt bee corpses had disturbed her profoundly, and for months she'd had to tread carefully lest she tread on a hidden sting.

"Look," she said testily, as it dive-bombed her left ear for the hundredth time, "do you mind?"

"Oh sorry *darling,*" it replied, giggling. "I didn't mean to make a pest of myself,"

"Well you are," she snapped. The bee dipped apologetically in the air, and Palli felt a small twinge of guilt. It occurred to her that this bee was probably related to the hive she'd had massacred, and that made her feel meaner than ever.

"Sorry. It's just been a *really* bad few weeks."

"Oh, sweetheart, *I'm* sorry. It's the whole mating season thing with me. You know how it is with insects; once that time of year comes round you simply can't help bothering other people at all!"

"He-Wolves," Palli said tartly, "are much the same,"

"*Are* they?" The bee settled on a nearby leaf, about level with Palli's nose. She took her time folding her wings away neatly, and continued.

"I've never talked to a wolf before. Are the he-wolves much like you?"

"No. They're a bootless, shifty bunch of ne'er-do-wells, most of whom never make it past adolescence it terms of mental development. What are your he-bees like? I hear they're useless"

There was a pause. Palli thought maybe she'd hit a nerve- maybe this bee was going through some romantic troubles. She pawed at the ground a little nervously.

"It's not *our* fault," said the bee after a moment.

"Sorry?"

"Well, the females are the ones who do all the work. They *take* it on themselves."

"Oh! You're a man."

"Of course I am! What did you think I was?"

"Well you did call me darling. I just thought you were, you know..."

The bee buzzed angrily.

"So? So what? I do *not* look like a woman, for goodness sake, look at this," and it did a funny sort of loop-the-loop. "Does that look like a sting to you? No!"

"Well..." Palli wrinkled her nose, "You all sort of look the same to me,"

"That, darling, is *prejudice,*"

"Oh."

Palli had to fight to keep her tale from curling between her legs in embarrassment, and the bee whirred its wings a few times in an affronted sort of way, but did not leave. The silence hung on between them, until Palli felt she had to break the tension.

"You really are as camp as anything you know," she said with a grin which only a wolf can give. It was a dangerous, roguish charming smile, and it worked.

"Darling, I'm *fabulous*, and so are you!"

"So... you don't have a sting?"

"No. Only the she-bees have stings."

"Oh. So... what do you do if you don't sting things or do work?"

"Mate,"

"Apart from that I mean."

"Die,"

"Really? That's it."

"Yeah."

"That's so unfair. I *wish* my life was that simple. I've got to raise my cubs, hunt, teach them how *not* to get shot by humans, plus their father is a *complete* non-entity. Not to mention I haven't had a fuck in *ages.* And your entire purpose in life is to screw for a living."

"Yeah... it's pretty simple,"

"Lucky,"

"Not really. Not all of us get to mate. And you know, the ones that do only do it once before our dicks fall off and eviscerate us,"

Palli blinked. "What does eviscerate mean?"

"Disembowel. Our guts fall out and we die,"

"Oh,"

"So why do you mate? Why don't you just stay home, and not do it,"

"It's kind of what we do. It's our purpose; it's what we're for."

"But if you *die-*"

"It doesn't matter really. Not in the long run. I guess it's about integrity. About doing what you can for your family, for your species. That's what you're doing isn't it?"

"No. I'm living for me,"

"Are you?"

"Yes! I look after my cubs because I love them! I'm a mother, it's what I do."

"So, you don't think your life would be easier if you didn't have them?"

"Well... yes... but that's not the point. I love them, that's why I do what I do."

"That must be nice for you." said the bee, though Palli thought she caught a hint of derision in his voice. After a moment he said

"I don't love anyone,"

"Not even your family?"

"What's family? The creatures born in the next cell, the ones who share some weird code you can't even see? No, I don't love them. But I love the Hive. I owe it my life, and it just so happens that someday soon it's going to collect on that debt."

"That's not fair,"

"Isn't it? At the end of the day isn't it what we'd all do if we had to. Family is an idea, and what's worth dying for other than an idea?"

"An individual?"

"One for one? Seems kinda silly,"

"It's not about the maths. It's about... people. It's about... doing what you can to stay alive, because you deserve it. Nothing matters other than that. The ground beneath your paws, the smell of the sunset. All the beauty of a battle wound, the poetry of sex and touch and sensation."

"Have much time for that with four cubs do you?"

"Well, no. But they'll be grown soon enough,"

"And in the meanwhile you might as well be me. I fuck and die. You died and became a mother, a glorified wetnurse. We all play a role, and we all sacrifice ourselves for it."

"Being a mother is who I *am*!" Palli growled

"Who were you before?"

"Me."

"Really?"

Palli shuffled her paws uncomfortably. Becoming a parent changes you, yes, but that's just natural. It doesn't make you any less of a wolf. True she hunted rats on occasion, which the Great Packs would have found utterly disgraceful. And- this she thought rather guiltily- her destruction of the beehive wasn't exactly in keeping with Jungle Law. But these days you do what you have to. You survive.

"I think it's sad. That a sad little fuck is more important to you than the rest of your life,"

"It's not like that for us. We don't enjoy it,"

"But... you can't just go off to your death like that!"

"I don't have a choice,"

"There's always a choice,"

The bee made no reply. Although it was still, Palli thought she could hear the buzzing of the whole hive at the edge of her imagination.

Still the bee said nothing. Palli felt a little squib of victory, and then quite suddenly she missed her children.

"I should go." she said. The bee said goodbye, somewhat morosely and she turned back through the jungle, relishing the sensation of the occasional ray of sun breaking through the canopy onto he face.

It must, she thought as she crashed through the forest, be a very disturbing life to live. To know that your entire purpose in life was to be accomplished in an instant, and then you would die. To watch the cubs grow really wasn't that bad of a deal after all.

Palli's den was in a cave at the foot of a stony hill. A tiny little entrance- you wouldn't have thought a wolf could fit through it. A shoebox of a place really. But home. Palli stood outside for a moment, nudging the side of the cave in gratitude. Between them she and the cubs probably knew every crevice of their little corner of the world. Creepers climbed all over, in and between the rocks, and when it rained the water collected just outside, so that they had easy access to drinking water. In time, perhaps, the cubs could help her in defending it, from the small creatures who tried to drink there. A sort of preliminary training. The thought of her freedom from them suddenly seemed less appealing, and she longed to nuzzle them, to lick and laugh with them, to answer Dharshana's questions, and listen to Kumeru's stories, or to run with her daughters under the moon and get into mischief with them, a joy which no Man can ever take away from a wolf.

Typically then, they all seemed to be asleep. All four of them at the same time, which *never* happened.

Suddenly she wondered how the bee had known she had four cubs. She hadn't told him.

It also occurred to her that the cave stank. Something powdery, and sweet, and acidic lingered in the air, like poison and drunken anger. It was horribly familiar.

She rounded a corner and looked into onto a shelf of rock and saw the cubs, and the echo of her howl scattered birds for miles around.

All four of them lay there, unnaturally still. Their sweet faces were puffed and swollen, weeping and stuck all around with vicious little stings, and there was fluid seeping from their eyelids and matting in the facefur.

All around in the darkness, stingless bees twitched, squirmed, and then died quietly and without complaint.

# Roses

Pink rose, like quivering flesh
Heavy with the carapaces
of vagabond bees

Begging to be let into the boudoir
A kind of perfumed suicide
A kind of sprint to the finish line

As if in dry oblivion
they will find something more
Atonement for bearing thorns perhaps
and the petals made worthwhile

# Stormverse

A dirge of disapproving clouds above
Pendulous, pregnant with hot rain
Down it in one- a shot of air,
a throat burning gulp of cloves
and ozone

It is a rebellion:
all summer long the world has been sweet
raising gentle orange groves,
honeyed apples black with flies
and bloody, pretty little hearts
which lie innocent in strawberry patches

Now black tempered earth fights back

Now the birds between the trees
are flapping, frantic shiny things
winging pointless airways to places safe
from brash lightning and scalding rain

Of course, they cannot escape

Creation quivers, scared as
silence crests
The landscape waits a second...
a second more

Razor bright the first drop falls
and the world is ravished.

# The Fruit Thief

Some sweet thing scooped
caressed
Honey, marshmallow, marzipan
Eased stickily from my breast
with our best times

I understand but do not care

You filched my plums in Armagnac
My rum soaked cherries, bauble bright
Plump pears for perry making

Now my fruit trees have bare branches

Old bread, cold meat, a square of cheese
these days may pass for adequate fare

# First Contact

Everyone remembers their first kiss. I always just figured I'd have more to remember about her. I thought my first kiss would be my first lover, someone I trusted, that we'd have a perfect moment and suddenly know we were in love, or could be with a little time. And I never expected it to work out in the long run. But I thought we'd love each other, and if that changed we'd be friends, soulmates.

Vicky and I met in Camden. My best friend at the time, Sooraya, introduced us. She said, as if it was obvious, that it was high time I got myself a girlfriend. Sooraya was like that. We'd go to parties at people's houses, and I'd stand next to her holding a WKD (she always asked for a sip) while she talked to boys, tilting her head to one side and playing coquettishly with a corner of her pale pink shayla.
So she introduced me to Vicky, a friend of her brother's girlfriend. I was a little resentful; I didn't *need* setting up. But I never managed to get good at saying no, so I agreed to meet her.

It was sunny outside Camden Town Tube station, and the sun was low in the sky so that its light was painting everyone in glorious, syrupy shades of sepia and the street smelled like melting butter from a waffle stand a little way off. When I saw them... when I saw *her.* She was walking towards me, and the sunlight caught her blond curls like the Hand of Midas, turning them into deep, lustrous gold. I will always remember that image, that first time I saw her, and how beautiful the world was for those few seconds. Of course, it's something of an invention. What happened later colours the way I remember this day, I know that. It may even have been a little overcast. It doesn't matter; our memories are what we make of them, unless there are photographs to prove otherwise, and even a photograph can tell different stories to different people.

Sooraya and her brother's girlfriend stayed with us for a little while, enough to go and look at some clothes. I didn't say much. Then they left, far too soon, and Vicky and I walked up to the Lock in silence. We leaned against the bridge, next to each other, and looked out at the horizon.

"Um... I'm sorry... I've forgotten your name,"

"It's William...Will".

"Sorry?"

"Will," I said a little louder. She smiled at me.

"It's beautiful, this place," she said, gesturing out at the boats, the water, the sky.

"Yeah, it is. I wish I had my camera,"

"Oh, yeah, you're a photographer,"

She turned to look at me, and her hand on the railing moved so that our little fingers were touching.

Seconds passed. It suddenly became very important that I showed her I was interested in her.

"Do you like photography?"

She nodded. "I like Mapplethorpe,"

I arched an eyebrow. "You do?"

"Not what you expected me to like?"

"Well, not really," I smiled. "I like him too,"

We kept looking at each other for a moment. I could feel the heat from her little finger on mine, and I twitched it involuntarily. Somehow it ended up on top of hers.

"You look really pretty at this time of day,"

She laughed. "The darker it gets the better I look!"

"No." I said firmly. Then I blushed hideously. Why had I said that? Very suddenly her finger was stroking mine, just a little motion, a repeated circle.

She smiled at me, her eyes flickering down to my lips for a fraction of a second. And then she did it again, for a little longer. And then, with her hand now resting on mine, she kissed me.

It was my first. This was *it*. Belatedly, I remembered reading somewhere that you were meant to close your eyes. Her lips were impossibly soft, moving with a gentleness which was almost hesitant. It was ecstasy. It was like feeling every nerve suddenly caressed, awoken. I barely moved for a second or two, and then I reciprocated, awkwardly, trying to copy, to convey the same feeling.

It lasted maybe two seconds, and then she moved her hand. When I opened my eyes I expected to see her face, looking at me with... something. But she was looking back over the Lock, her face beautiful and fine boned and unreadable. I followed her gaze.

"Sorry," she softly. She still didn't look at me. I imagined ghosting a graceful hand over her cheek like a rom-com leading man, turning her face to mine and whispering "I'm not" before bringing her in for another, more perfect kiss as the sun set and the titles scrolled, the world leaving us to some sort of happy ending.

"Why?" I said jerkily. Was that really my voice? I sounded brash, vulnerable, scared.

"It was just a kiss," I blurted. Where a few moments ago my body had been alive it now felt remarkably like the bottom had dropped out of my stomach, leaving the vital parts of myself to land wetly on the pavement. She twisted her face oddly, in discomfort, licked her lips.

She didn't say anything for the longest time.

# Sweat

Hush!
Under the covers of sweat and night
For an instant
There's you.
There's me.

There is the sulphurous pit!
Darling! Fall in?
I didn't bring trunks.

I kissed you first under cover of dark
there I loved first the jut of your hands
Your spine

Under dark you proposed
confessed loves, fears and woes
Under dark, when we sweat
You are mine

# Scarlet Is Your Colour

Under the moon
       (she does not look)
I pluck a pearl from
       your throat
I suck the poison from
       your wounds
I fuck you the way
       you like

To be taken, to know (Oh, God!)
that soon the wind will fall away, and we will fly to...
       -Sorry. How else to say it?
How else to name the things we do?
Like two vast continents of
       paper and thought (all a life really is)
Reduced to flesh
       to less than this
Weird covenant.

Around us the flowers spray
       strange juice
They are your favourites. Exquisite and scarlet.
       you are

Not mine.
I do not own the days of your life
I do not get to the folded pip
       of memories, Galette des Rois
in your grandmother's home
I cannot smell her perfume

But I still hold you

arms, legs, chest
Minutiae, kilograms, molecules
I still feel your breath from real, pink lungs


It is something, it is hair and skin
        and bone.
You do not belong to anyone, nor do I.
When you die your
        tissues will degrade.
I cannot hold you once you have gone.
I cannot kiss you once you have gone

Scarlet flowers are the ones
        you like best
Lie to the moon, the newspapers.
Tell them you are mine and
        I am yours
And we will be alright.
Tell the untruths nice and blithely.
Shh! I know; there is no scarlet if
**there is no light.**

# Mania 2011

I lie on my bed
imbibing air and lizards
I feel them
 slithering down my throat
like fingers dry with snakescale skin
and disease

A scream lasts impossible epochs
A scream takes work to perfect
anything less than flesh to grinding stone
leaves desire
which must be exorcised
like a demon

Like an unclean thing, curled
between the pelvic bones,
twisting sinews into mad arabesques
for its own sick amusement

The kingdom and the glory
are magnificent inside my head:
perverse and utterly ridiculous.

I scratch at my skin in the night
begging to be born anew
There are worse things than death
or truth, or banality
There are worse things than we
dare to imagine

Mania is one of these

Printed in Great Britain
by Amazon.co.uk, Ltd.,
Marston Gate.